UNIVERSE to GOD

The Ancient Wisdom of Sages For Children

Anuradha Adarsh

PRACTICE BOOK

Universe to God

by

Anuradha Adarsh

BLUEROSE PUBLISHERS

India | U.K.

Copyright © Anuradha Adarsh 2023

All rights reserved by author. No part of this publication may be reproduced, stored in a retrieval system or transmitted in any form or by any means, electronic, mechanical, photocopying, recording or otherwise, without the prior permission of the author. Although every precaution has been taken to verify the accuracy of the information contained herein, the publisher assumes no responsibility for any errors or omissions. No liability is assumed for damages that may result from the use of information contained within.

BlueRose Publishers takes no responsibility for any damages, losses, or liabilities that may arise from the use or misuse of the information, products, or services provided in this publication.

For permissions requests or inquiries regarding this publication, please contact:

BLUEROSE PUBLISHERS
www.BlueRoseONE.com
info@bluerosepublishers.com
+91 8882 898 898
+4407342408967
ISBN: 978-93-5819-800-3
Cover design: Muskan Sachdeva
Typesetting: Rohit
First Edition: December 2023

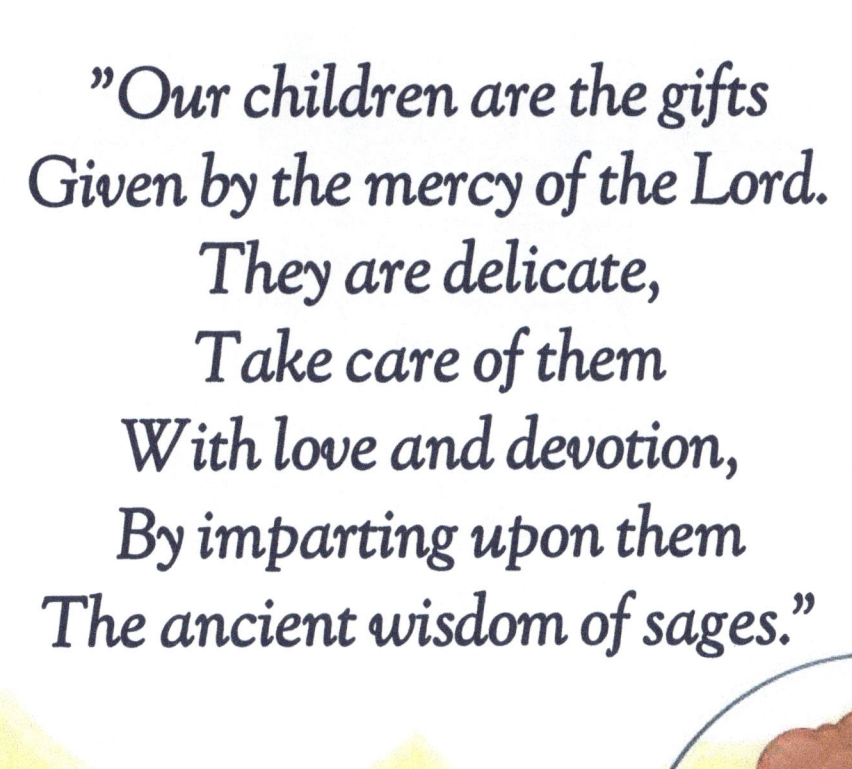

"Our children are the gifts
Given by the mercy of the Lord.
They are delicate,
Take care of them
With love and devotion,
By imparting upon them
The ancient wisdom of sages."

Name : ....
Age : ....
Class : ....

Universe to God is our first s e r i e s this
is Practice Book of our first series.

Instruction - Write With Sketch pen in different Colours.

Writing 2 pages per week is great,
But per day 1 page is the best.

Benefits of colouring for kids:-

Develops fine motor skills

Encourages patience and relaxation

Helps with concentration

Assists with language development

Further handwriting skills

Encourage colour recognition

Preparation for school

Boost their confidence

Help relieve stress

Promote creativity

Our Prayer
I am a shrine of Lord - God is in me

I Am		I Am
PEACE		PEACE
PURE		PURE
TRUE		TRUE

My self
I am a shrine of Lord - God is in me
I am peace pure and truth
Aham Brahmasmi
Aham Brahmasmi
Aham Brahmasmi

Thanks to God
Thank you, God. You made a beautiful universe for us.
Thank you, God. For creating the earth for us to live on.
Thank you, God. You made scriptures, which gives knowledge of the whole universe

Prayer to God
Oh God give me the strength. I do all my work with

Peace, pure and truth.
Oh God, I receive correct knowledge from all directions.
Oh God, I receive noble thoughts from all directions.
Oh God, guide me to the right goal for my life.
Oh God I live happily with my family...

Ancient Wisdom of the sages   :   Do the prayer 2 times, in the morning and night

Chanting OM, Writing OM, Listening OM gives Concentration.

Chanting OM, Writing OM, Listening OM gives Concentration.

ॐ ॐ ॐ ॐ ॐ ॐ ॐ

Chanting OM, Writing OM, Listening OM gives Concentration.

Om Mani Pad Me Hum

Listening to Mantra gives Peace and at the same time, it Heals.

Om Mani Pad Me Hum

Listening to Mantra gives Peace and at the same time, it Heals.

ॐ भूर् भुवः स्वः।
तत्स वितु वरेण्यं।
भर्गो देवस्य धीमहि।
धियो यो नः प्रचो दयात्॥

It is prayer to God thanks for everything.

ॐ भूर् भुवः स्वः।
तत्स वितु वरेण्यं।
भर्गो देवस्य धीमहि।
धियो यो नः प्रचो दयात्॥

It is prayer to God thanks for everything.

Om   Bhur   Bhuvah   Swah
Tat   Savitur   Varenyam
Bhargo Devasya Dheemahi
Dhiyo Yo Nah Prachodayaat

It is prayer to God thanks for everything.

Om Bhur Bhuvah Swah
Tat Savitur Varenyam
Bhargo Devasya Dheemahi
Dhiyo Yo Nah Prachodayaat

It is prayer God gives us Wisdom.

I am a shrine of Lord.
God is in me.

My daily prayer.

I am a shrine of Lord.
God is in me.

My daily prayer.

मैं भगवान का मंदिर हूँ
भगवान मेरे अंदर है

My daily prayer.

मैं भगवान का मंदिर हूँ
भगवान मेरे अंदर है

My daily prayer.

I am Pure, Peace and Truth

My daily prayer.

I am Pure, Peace and Truth

My daily prayer.

Aham Brahmasmi Aham Brahmasmi

Mahavakaya.

Aham Brahmasmi Aham Brahmasmi

Mahavakaya.

मैं शुद्ध, शांत और सत्य हूँ

My daily prayer.

मैं शुद्ध, शांत और सत्य हूँ

My daily prayer.

Om I am Generosity

Ma I am Ethics

Ni I am Patience

Om mani padma hum mantra is full of affermations.

I am Pad Perseverance

Me I am Concentration

Hum I am Wisdom

Om mani padma hum mantra is full of affermations.

Om Mani Pad Me Hum

_____

_____

_____

_____

_____

_____

_____

_____

_____

_____

_____

Listening to Mantra gives Peace and at the same time, it Heals.

Om Mani Pad Me Hum

Listening to Mantra gives Peace and at the same time, it Heals.

ॐ भूर् भुवः स्वः।

तत्स वितु वरेण्यं।

भर्गो देवस्य धीमहि।

धियो यो नः प्रचो दयात्॥

It is prayer to God thanks for everything.

ॐ भूर् भुवः स्वः।

तत्स वितु वरेण्यं।

भर्गो देवस्य धीमहि।

धियो यो नः प्रचो दयात्॥

It is prayer to God thanks for everything.

Om Bhur Bhuvah Swah
Tat Savitur Varenyam
Bhargo Devasya Dheemahi
Dhiyo Yo Nah Prachodayaat

It is prayer to God thanks for everything.

Om Bhur Bhuvah Swah
Tat Savitur Varenyam
Bhargo Devasya Dheemahi
Dhiyo Yo Nah Prachodayaat

It is prayer God gives us Wisdom.

I am a shrine of Lord.
God is in me.

My daily prayer.

I am a shrine of Lord.

God is in me.

My daily prayer.

मैं भगवान का मंदिर हूँ
भगवान मेरे अंदर है

My daily prayer.

मैं भगवान का मंदिर हूँ
भगवान मेरे अंदर है

My daily prayer.

I am Pure, Peace and Truth

My daily prayer.

I am Pure, Peace and Truth

My daily prayer.

Aham Brahmasmi Aham Brahmasmi

Mahavakaya.

Aham Brahmasmi Aham Brahmasmi

Mahavakaya.

Namaste   Namaste   Namaste

Namaste   Namaste   Namaste

_____

_____

_____

_____

_____

_____

_____

_____

_____

_____

Om I am Generosity

Ma I am Ethics

Ni I am Patience

Om mani padma hum mantra is full of affermations.

I am Pad Perseverance

Me I am Concentration

Hum I am Wisdom

Om mani padma hum mantra is full of affermations.

Om Mani Pad Me Hum

Om mani padma hum mantra is full of affermations.

Mantra

A mantra is a poetic revelation received by human sages during a state of deep concentration.

The essential power of the mantra is to make us see the world or think beyond our senses.

If we remember our mantra, we are free from many things, like being jealous, hatred, anger, negativity.

Nothing will affect us.

But remember the mantra when we are silent.

Remember our mantra with love.

Mantra is like an atomic power

If we are honestly relying on our mantra, it will sooner or later lead us to the highest peak.

Our mantra is our real friend in the world.

www.ingramcontent.com/pod-product-compliance
Lightning Source LLC
LaVergne TN
LVHW070535070526
838199LV00075B/6781